Taekwondo Kids

Dornemann / Rumpf

Meyer & Meyer Sport

Original Title: Taekwondo Kids – Weißgurt bis Gelbgrüngurt
© Meyer & Meyer Verlag, 2006

British Library Cataloguing in Publication Data
A catalogue record for this book is available from the British Library

Dornemann/Rumpf
Taekwondo Kids – From White Belt to Yellow/Green Belt
Oxford: Meyer & Meyer Sport (UK) Ltd., 2007
ISBN: 978-1-84126-214-7

© 2007 by Meyer & Meyer Sport (UK) Ltd.
Aachen, Adelaide, Auckland, Budapest, Graz, Johannesburg,
New York, Olten (CH), Oxford, Singapore, Toronto
Member of the World
Sports Publishers' Association (WSPA)
www.w-s-p-a.org
Printed and bound by: B.O.S.S Druck und Medien GmbH, Germany
ISBN: 978-1-84126-214-7
E-Mail: verlag@m-m-sports.com
www.m-m-sports.com

Contents

Acknowledgement

We would like to thank all those Taekwondo colleagues, friends and acquaintances, who have helped and supported us in the production of our book "Taekwondo Kids". In particular we would like to thank Willi Kloss (9th Dan WTF), Thomas Behrendt (5th Dan WTF), Christian Böcker (2nd Dan WTF) and Beate Füssel (2nd Dan WTF) for all the tips and review of the manuscript.

Our special thanks goes out to all children practicing Taekwondo and who train for years in this Martial Art and who work at it untiringly, both mentally and physically. Through our training work with children, our understanding for the Martial Arts and human behavior has been deepened.

Together we have learned.

"Dear Taekwondo Kids"

This book places a guide to practical exercises into your hands and this should lead you along the way to learning the Korean Martial Art. It is common for anyone practicing Taekwondo to have questions crop up while learning and exercising the various points. Am I doing everything right? What purpose does this particular technique serve? What must I know and be able to do for my next belt grading? It is not only the beginners, who ask this kind of question. On the contrary, advanced students and even the Masters ask them as well. Irrespective of the point you have reached, there is always something new to learn.

If you have got questions while you are training, then your instructor or trainer is there for you to answer them and help you. Sometimes there are also questions that crop up after your training or while you are practicing at home. Because your trainer is not there to answer them, it is good to have a different source to help you with them, like in the form of a practical handbook. So that you aren't left out in the cold with your questions, so to speak, we have written this book for you. Here we hope that you can find all the important sought after answers, tips and encouragement.

In the first instance, this book is an accompaniment to your actual training. Of course, if you haven't yet started your training in a school or club, you can get your first impressions and important facts about Taekwondo from this book. However, you must not get the impression that you can learn a Martial Art from a book and without the assistance of an instructor. It would be like saying that you could be a professional soccer player because you had watched so many championship games on TV. But, unfortunately it is not as easy as that. If you haven't started practicing Taekwondo yet and this book has given you an appetite to learn more, seek out and visit a club or school in your neighborhood.

Whether you want to browse through the subject first of all, or whether the bug has already bitten you, we wish you all success while practicing Taekwondo.

This book contains everything worth knowing for the beginner from White belt to Yellow/Green belt in this Korean Martial Art. The techniques are covered in accordance with the rules laid down by the "World Taekwondo Federation" (WTF) including the **poomsae** exercise forms practiced in the WTF.

The individual exercises and techniques will be shown and explained to you by our "Taekwondo Kids". Each of the children in this book represents a particular belt grading. Each child describes the techniques applicable to his particular belt grade and these are the ones, which it is necessary to learn for the test for the next grade belt. In the following pages we introduce the individual Taekwondoin (the term used for someone practicing Taekwondo).

Before we get going with the exercises, you will be able to read a chapter about "The History of Taekwondo", which contains quite a lot of the essential facts about this Korean Martial Art, e.g., where and when Taekwondo came into existence and what it is used for.

Descriptions of actual exercises follow on from the last theoretical part and at the end of the book you will find an appendix with diagrams, a technical vocabulary and other additional details.

You can read through the book from the beginning to the end or, on the other hand, you can start from a point that interests you most. The sections on your particular belt grade can be found quite simply by referring to the color code on the edge of the pages (or you can simply refer to the 'Contents' section at the front of the book).

And now . . . have lots of fun with the Taekwondo Kids and we wish you success with the exercises.

The Taekwondo Kids

Kira, Mike, Joanne, Farid and Suko are all friends, who train in the same Taekwondo club. They have been training for different lengths of time and therefore have different belt grades. They are going to show you in this book which techniques you need to take for your next grading test.

Kira is 9 years old and has been practicing Taekwondo only for a short while. She will show you the techniques necessary for the first grading test for the White/Yellow Belt (9ᵗʰ **kup**).

Mike is 12 and has already been in the group for a few months. He is getting ready to take the grading test for his Yellow Belt (8ᵗʰ **kup**).

Joanne, Mike's sister, is 11 years old and will shortly be taking the test for her Yellow/Green Belt (7th **kup**).

Farid, 10 years old, has already got his Yellow/Green Belt. You will find the techniques that are needed for his Green Belt grading test in the next volume. In this book, he is assisting the others in their exercises.

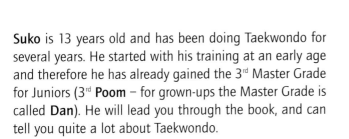

Suko is 13 years old and has been doing Taekwondo for several years. He started with his training at an early age and therefore he has already gained the 3rd Master Grade for Juniors (3rd **Poom** – for grown-ups the Master Grade is called **Dan**). He will lead you through the book, and can tell you quite a lot about Taekwondo.

The History of Taekwondo

For ages, people all over the world have been sparring and battling with each other, whether it was the young, who wanted to measure their strength through wrestling or whether it was to establish which was the leading tribe. Sometime or other, people began to refine the techniques of these fights and build a system out of them. Using this principle the first type of Martial Art was formed. With the introduction of the firearm in the western world, many of these Martial Arts went lost. However, in many of the countries in Asia, Martial Arts live on and over the centuries have even developed further.

Drawings from ancient Korean reliefs and graves

In Korea, paintings and drawings in burial chambers and on graves depict the forerunner of the Taekwondo Martial Art. In those days, the Chinese influence of the Han-Dynasty (205 BC – 220 AD) became increasingly weaker and three kingdoms were formed: Silla, Koguryo and Paeche. In Silla, the smallest of the kingdoms, a youth movement – the Hwa-Rang - was formed, which hunted, practiced religious beliefs and customs and exercised in self-defense. However, also in the other kingdoms, Taekwondo was being practiced under other names – Subyokta, Subak, Kwonbaek, Byon and Tagyok.

In 918 BC, the three kingdoms were united under the name of Koryo (Korea). Martial Art began to slip into the background and more and more, authors and poets became popular and received better patronage.

Martial Arts came back into its own following a State revolt. In those days, the Martial Art Subakhi was widely popular amongst the population and it was systematically cultivated. During the Yi-Dynasty (1392-1910), the exam for higher civil servants included, amongst other things, a successful fight against three competitors.

In 1910, the Japanese occupied the country and Korean Martial Arts were forbidden until Korea was liberated.

In 1955, several styles of Martial Arts i.e., Ji Do Kwan, Mu Do Kwan or Oh Do Kwan were fused together and were given the unified name of Taekwondo.

In 1973, the first World Championships were held in Seoul, Korea and the World Taekwondo Federation (WTF) was set up.

In 1976, the European Taekwondo Union (ETU) was founded.

A Part I:

White Belt (10th kup)

1 "Hello Friends"

My name is Suko. I'm 13 years old and like my chosen Martial Art – Taekwondo – I come from Korea. I have been practicing Taekwondo (TKD) since I was five. I have got as far as the 3rd **Poom**. What this means, I will tell you later. My Martial Art goes back over 2000 years with its traditions. People have always wrestled with each other and romped about with each other both when playing about as well as in training. Earlier, the old types of Martial Art were called Subak or Taekyon. It was first in 1955 that various different schools got together under the name of Taekwondo. In this word the **'tae'** means all the 'foot techniques' and **'kwon'** means all the 'hand techniques' while **'do'** means the 'way'. The latter part-word stands for the physical and spiritual development, which comes about from many years of training.

Two years ago, I emigrated from Korea together with my mother and father, who is a University guest professor.

Through my chosen Martial Art, I very quickly made lots of friends. Many of them wanted to get to know about Taekwondo, therefore my father trained with us. We have a training hall **(dojang)** at the University where we train twice a week.

For the training sessions we wear a Taekwondo suit called the **'dobok'**. If you have just started with Taekwondo or are just getting a taste of the sport, it is sufficient for the first few times to wear other sports clothing. However, as soon as you have decided to take up Taekwondo seriously, you should get yourself a **dobok**. At the very least you will need it for your first grading test.

The basic color of the **dobok** is white. This implies that that the student is like an unfinished drawing or like an empty glass, into which fresh water (i.e., knowledge) has yet to be poured. Only the Master may wear something a little black (e.g., the collar), because his knowledge and ability is greater than that of the student. Otherwise his uniform is basically white, because one never finishes the learning process.

A belt, called the 'ty', is worn with the **dobok**. For beginners, this is also colored white. For higher grades of students it is colored differently with each color showing which Taekwondo grade **(kup)** each of the students possesses.

To start with you have to learn how to tie the belt properly. The simplest way is to lay the **ty** out so that both of the ends just lay over each other – the belt must not become twisted. You lay the middle of the belt at the point where it is folded onto your stomach and pull the ends round to the rear behind your waist. Where the strips of the belt cross over each other you then bring the ends back towards the front. It is important that the belt lays smoothly over the **dobok** without being twisted. The ends of the belt at the front must be the same length. You now bring one end of the belt over the other strip and through under it, and using the upper strip of belt, you tie a knot.

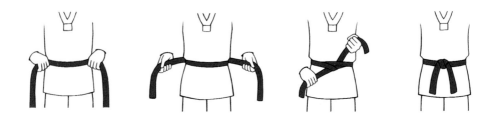

Tying the belt is not so easy for a beginner. Therefore, for the first few times you should let someone show you how to do it.

When getting ready for training, as soon as you have finished tying the belt, this means that you are now prepared for the upcoming training and that you are now only concentrating on Taekwondo. When you are wearing the belt, you should not eat, drink or chew gum. After the training session, before you do anything else, you must take the belt off.

When you enter the training hall, you bow out of respect and politeness towards the others in order to show that you have your mind on the training.

When training begins, we all line up in front of the trainer **(sabum)**, starting with the highest belt and then filling in down to the beginner.

The beginner has a White Belt (10th **kup**) because he only knows a little or even nothing at all yet.

As a sign that the trainee is on the way towards the Yellow Belt the ty has a stripe, for example Mike has a yellow stripe (9th **kup**) on his White Belt.

Joanne already has the Yellow Belt (8th **kup**). Yellow stands for earth. Earth is necessary for plants to grow. Thus the Yellow Belt stands, figuratively speaking, for the willingness of the student to grow in knowledge.

The second Yellow Belt has a green stripe (7th **kup**).

Green (6th **kup**) stands for the plants, which grow in the earth. This means that the Green Belt also stands for the knowledge about Taekwondo that is now 'growing' in the student.

For the second Green Belt, one gets a blue stripe (5th **kup**).

The next step is the Blue Belt (4th **kup**). It symbolizes the sky, towards which the plants on the earth grow.

For the second Blue Belt one gets a red stripe (3rd **kup**).

Following on is the Red Belt (2nd **kup**), which symbolizes that something special is present, hence the red signal color.

As the last belt for students, comes the Red Belt with a black stripe (1st **kup**). This is the last step for students prior to the Junior Master Grade (**Poom**).

For each grade of belt, one has to take a test and show that you have mastered the techniques.

For the 10th **kup**, nowadays you don't have to take a test any more. It used to be that you had to be able to put the **dobok** together properly and tie the belt correctly and describe how one behaves correctly in the training hall (**dojang**).

2   Behavior in the Training Hall (Dojang)

There are certain rules on how a Taekwondoin should behave in the **dojang**. These rules, which also contain points about politeness and humbleness, not only cover behavior in your own training hall, but also particularly when visiting other **dojangs** and most often outside the **dojang**.

When you enter the **dojang**, you stop, place the feet together and incline the body forward in a bow with the arms held down by the side of the body. By bowing, you show respect on the one hand for all the Taekwondoin present in the training hall, and on the other hand you show that you are ready to want to train seriously and put your full concentration into it.

At the beginning of the training session everyone lines up in front of the instructor as per his or her belt colors. Then on the command "Pay attention, Greetings!" **(charyot kyongne)** everyone bows as before when you entered the training hall.

This second bow shows that you are paying respect to your instructor and all the other students in the hall.

Once you have entered the training hall you should not speak anymore, so that you are able to concentrate and not disturb the others.

When doing exercises with a partner you should go about it quietly, show respect and always act fairly. In order to endorse this behavior, you also bow to your partner before and after the exercise.

The white training uniform should always be clean, and, when being worn, properly adjusted together with a correctly tied belt.
All students are, in the first instance, equal and are distinguished only by the color of the belt (= at different stages).

At the end of training, everyone lines up again and bows towards the instructor **(sabum)**.

When leaving the hall, as a final action, you bow again.

The training uniform and belt **(ty)** should only be worn for training. The belt should only be worn in conjunction with the training uniform and you should then not eat or drink when wearing it.

In addition, you should keep to the following rules:

1.) Humbleness
Don't overrate your performance and don't brag in front of the other students.

2.) Politeness
Always behave courteously towards your classmates and be friendly.

3.) Respect
Show respect towards your instructor and all your classmates. After all you have shown the outward sign of wanting to do this by bowing.

4.) Fairness
When doing exercises with a partner always act fairly and without any ulterior motives in mind. Unsporting behavior is not welcome here.

5.) Self-control
Never show your temper when training, even when you think you have been unfairly treated yourself. Always arrive punctually and always behave in a disciplined manner in the training hall.

6.) Patience
Even when some exercises are repeated often and when you have to wait sometimes a long time until the next belt-grading test is due, always show patience. Your patience and tenacity will pay off in the end.

7.) Helpfulness
Always be ready to help other students during the training. Perhaps you can even help the instructor to integrate new students into the group.

8.) Openness
Always be open with your classmates and don't engage in boasting (see Humbleness).

3   Warming up

Each training session begins with a warm-up program. First, we begin with a training session of cardiovascular exercises e.g., running or hopping on the spot. Then come stretching exercises. Because there are so many possibilities to structure the warm-up program, and every instructor has his own methods, we will not try to depict any particular exercises here. After the warm-up come the proper exercises: blocks, strikes and kicks.

4 What You Already Know

In the section about the White Belt you have already learnt quite a number of things that you have to know as a basis for Taekwondo. You know how to tie the **ty** and how to behave during training and you also have learnt a number of Korean terms. So that you can remember them easier, they are included at the end of this first section laid out so that you can see them altogether. At the end of the following main sections of the book, you will always find the latest terms laid out so you can learn them step by step.

As a beginner, you don't have to memorize all of them yet. It is, however, a good thing if you begin to try and memorize them as early as possible, because as an advanced student you will have to know them in any case. Why particularly Korean terminology? They are used by Taekwondoin throughout the world and if you have learnt them, then wherever you practice Taekwondo you will understand which techniques are meant, whether you are in France, Australia or Brazil. Moreover, in other Martial Arts, whether they stem from China, Japan or somewhere else, the terminology used is always taken from the language of the country of origin.

If you want to look up and refer to a word, you will find an Appendix with a vocabulary of words that have appeared in Volume 1 in alphabetical order at the end. When trying to pronounce the Korean terms, simply speak them phonetically. Also, for now you should read the note about pronunciation at the beginning of the 'Vocabulary' Section in the Appendix at the end of the book.

You should start to learn to count in Korean – at least the first ten numbers. You can practice them on the next page.

5 Korean Terminology I

dojang	training hall
dobok	training uniform
ty	belt
kup	belt grade
poom	Master grade for Juniors
dan	Master grade for grown-ups
sabum	trainer, instructor

Important Commands:

charyot kyongne	Pay attention, Greetings!
chunbi	Get ready! Adopt a starting position
sijak	Begin!
guman	end of the exercise, or end of being ready

Numbers:

hana	one
dul	two
set	three
net	four
dasot	five
yosot	six
Igup	seven
yodol	eight
ahop	nine
yol	ten

B Part II:

White/Yellow Belt (9th kup)

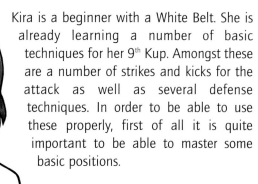

Kira is a beginner with a White Belt. She is already learning a number of basic techniques for her 9th Kup. Amongst these are a number of strikes and kicks for the attack as well as several defense techniques. In order to be able to use these properly, first of all it is quite important to be able to master some basic positions.

The Korean word for 'position' is **sogi**. The individual positions use this word e.g., **moa sogi, kima sogi** or **ap sogi**. (What these positions look like, Kira will show us in the following pages). Other positions use the word **gubi** instead of the word sogi (e.g., **ap gubi** or **dwit gubi**). This word means 'bent'. It is used for the positions where the knee is bent sharply.

1 Positions

moa sogi (closed position)

You stand upright with both of your feet together.

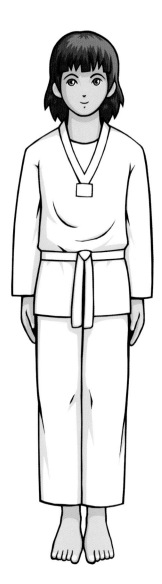

Feet together

pyonhi sogi (parallel position)

Place your left leg outwards until your feet are shoulder width apart. The toes point forward.

B

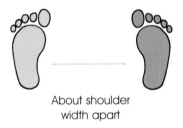

About shoulder
width apart

chunbi sogi or gibbon chunbi (ready position)

Stand in the **pyonhi sogi** position and place your fists in front of the belt so that they are about the width of a fist apart and are pointing towards each other.

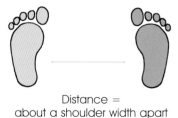

Distance =
about a shoulder width apart

kima sogi (saddle position, feet parallel)

Standing in the **pyonhi sogi** position you place your left leg outwards until there are about two shoulder widths between your feet. The feet are parallel and the toes are pointing forwards. The knees are angled sharply and are pointing slightly outwards.

B

Distance = about two
shoulder widths apart

chuchum sogi (riding position, feet splayed out)

This position is similar to the **kima sogi** position, but this time the knees are not so sharply bent and the feet must not be parallel. In many schools and clubs **kima sogi** is seldom used and **chuchum sogi** is taught.

Distance = almost
two shoulder widths apart

ap sogi (short step forward)

One foot is in front of the other and about half a shoulder width apart from the other foot. The toes are pointing forward and the knees are slightly bent. The upper body is upright.

B

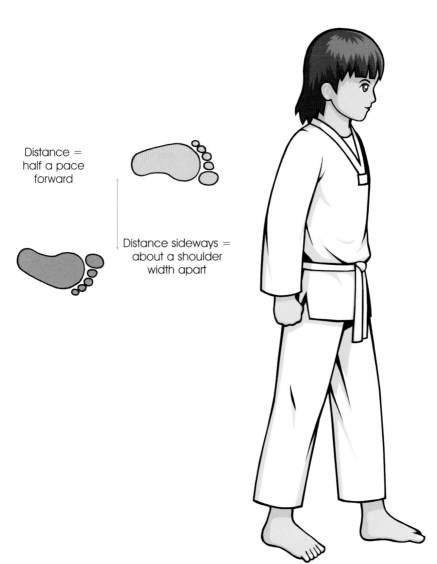

Distance = half a pace forward

Distance sideways = about a shoulder width apart

ap gubi (long step forward)

You are standing in the **pyonhi sogi** position. You take a pace forward about one and a half shoulders width between the two feet. The forward knee is bent so that it is above the heel. The rear leg is stretched and the rear foot is turned slightly outwards.

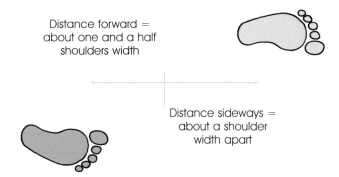

Distance forward =
about one and a half
shoulders width

Distance sideways =
about a shoulder
width apart

In the positions that Kira has learnt up until now, the weight of the body is equally spread on both legs. Many of the techniques can be used starting from these positions.

Kira will show you the foot techniques next.

2 Foot Techniques

ap chagi (forward kick)

You are standing in the **ap gubi** position and bring the rear leg up into a bent position. Watch the position of your feet at this point: The toes are lifted up and the instep is stretched out. Now you kick the lower leg forwards until the leg is fully stretched out. Afterwards, you pull the lower leg back and place the foot down in front. You hit the target with the ball of your foot (**ap chuk**).

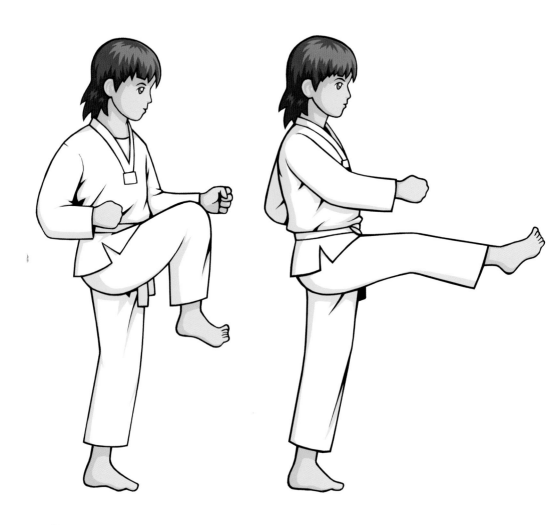

naeryo chagi (kick upwards)

From the **ap gubi** position, you swing the outstretched leg upwards, keeping your upper body up straight. Toes and instep are both tensed up. At the highest point, you pull the outstretched leg sharply downwards again and a little to the outside. You hit the target with the heel (**dwit kumchi**).

yop chagi (sideways kick with the foot)

You are standing in **kima** or **chuchum sogi** and bring the left leg up behind the right leg. When you are standing firmly, you lift up the right knee until the thigh is parallel with the ground. The lower leg is angled. You now kick the leg out until the upper body and the leg are stretched out. Just imagine that there is a tightened rope between your bottom and the target. Your heel moves along the rope until it reaches the target. Watch out that the foot of your standing leg twists a little. The upper body bends so that it is sloping in line with the ground. You hit the target with the outside edge of the foot (**balnal**). After that you pull your leg back again, straighten up and place your leg into the **kima** or **chuchum sogi** position.

Tip:

All the techniques are described here being done from a particular position. Later on you will do these techniques from other positions. This is the case with all of the techniques that follow in this book. However, practice them first of all using the positions described here.

4 Defense Techniques

hechyo arae makki (double wedge block in the lower zone)

In the **ap gubi** position bring your arms up crossed in front of the chest. The backs of the hand are pointing forwards. The arms are then brought down and outwards in a movement to the sides, during which you breathe out. The block is made with the upper side of your forearms.

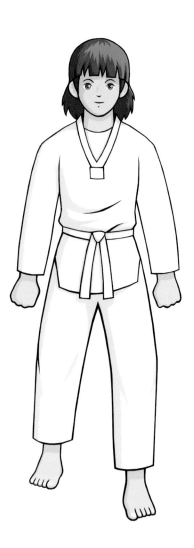

arae makki (block in the lower zone)

You are standing in the **ap gubi** position. The arm on the side of the rear leg is stretched out in front of the body. The other arm is brought up high onto the opposite shoulder. The arm is now brought sharply downwards with force until it is a fist width away from the thigh of the forward leg and the attack is blocked using the upper edge of the forearm. At the same time, the other fist is brought back onto the hip and at the end of the movement, turned so that the back of the fist is pointing at the ground.

olgul makki (block in the upper zone)

Bring both arms up crossed in front of the chest. The arm on the side of the forward leg is on the inside close to the body. The inside of the fist is facing the upper body and is held at shoulder height. The other arm provides forward protection with the back of the fist facing towards you. You now bring the inside arm up above your head. Your upper arm is almost level with your ear. The forearm is held up slightly at a diagonal. At the same time the other arm is pulled back onto the hip. The inside of the fist is pointing upwards.

There is also a variation where the blocking arm is brought in from the outside instead of from the inside.

pakkat palmok momdong an makki (block in the middle zone using the outer side of the forearm inwards)

The arm on the side of the forward leg is brought up across the chest onto the shoulder while the arm on the other side is held out diagonally forward of the body. The block is made with the forward leg arm warding any possible attack away inwards. At the same time the other arm is brought back onto the hip.

pakkat palmok momdong pakkat makki (block in the middle zone using the outer side of the forearm outwards)

Both arms are crossed and held up in front of the chest. The fist of the inside blocking arm should be over the other shoulder. The inside of the fist is facing you. The inside edge of the other arm is facing away from you. You twist the fist round so that you are looking at the back of the fist. The other fist is brought down onto the hip with the inside of the fist facing upwards. You block until the attack just passes by your body.

Here, also, there is the possibility that the blocking arm is not brought inwards but is brought round from the outside.

5 Attack Techniques

Kira will now show you the punch (jumok jirugi) – an attack technique carried out with the hand.

jumok jirugi (punching)

You are standing in the **kima sogi** position. The left arm is stretched forward with the back of the fist facing upwards. The right fist (with the inside of the fist facing upwards) is held on the hip. You now punch forward at the middle of the body until the arm is nearly fully stretched out. At the same time the other hand is brought back onto the hip. At the end of the movement both fists are turned over so that the back of the right fist is facing upwards and the inside of the left fist is facing upwards. The movement has to be done quickly and with force. The punch hits the target using the two forward knuckles.

Exercises

Do the punching action alternately with the left and the right fist. Pay attention to the way the fists have to be turned. Especially at the beginning it often occurs that when pulling the fist back, you forget to turn it over. If you practice it often, this mistake will soon not happen any more.

After doing a simple straight punching action, do exercises with a double punching action. To do this you punch forward with both fists alternately and then quickly repeat it again without taking a pause in between. Watch out that you do the turnover of the fist again. The double punching action is called **dubon jirugi**.

Try the punching action also in another position e.g., from an **ap sogi** position. As you do each punch, move forward one pace in the position. In this exercise, you can do the punch with the arm that is on the same side as the forward leg. This punching action is called **bandae jirugi**. Once you have practiced this technique going forward, do the same exercise using the arm that is on the same side as the rear leg. When you do this punching action it is called **baro jirugi**. You can see these actions in the sketches at the bottom of the last two pages.

So that you don't get confused with the description that follows, we call the punching action simply by the term **jumok jirugi** irrespective of which leg it is done from. This comes automatically from the description.

Kihap

When you carry out the punching action you shout out as loud as you can. This cry is called **kihap**. It serves to give you energy and show your determination. Besides that it increases your pluck and intimidates your opponent. The cry of **kihap** also helps you to think about your breathing. For each technique you must breathe out, otherwise the action will have no power. By making a cry, you automatically have to breathe out and therefore cannot forget to do so.

Tip: When practicing the double punching action such as **dubon jirugi**, you only make the cry when you have completed the last action.

6 Korean Terminology II

Here we repeat all the Korean terms for the techniques that you have learnt for the 9th **kup**.

moa sogi	closed position
kima sogi	saddle position
ap sogi	short step forward
ap gubi	long step forward
chunbi	Get ready! Adopt a starting position.
pyonhi sogi	parallel position
chuchum sogi	riding position, feet splayed out
ap chagi	forward kick
naeryo chagi	kick upwards
yop chagi	sideways kick with the foot
olgul	upper zone
momdong	middle zone
arae	lower zone
arae makki	block in the lower zone
hechyo arae makki	double wedge block in the lower zone
olgul makki	block in the upper zone
pakkat palmok momdong an makki	block in the middle zone using the outer side of the forearm inwards
pakkat palmok momdong pakkat makki	block in the middle zone using the outer side of the forearm outwards
jumok jirugi	punching
dubon jirugi	double punching action
bandae jirugi	punching action on the forward leg side
baro jirugi	punching action on the rear leg side
kihap	attack cry
ap chuk	ball of the foot
balnal	outside edge of the foot
dwit kumchi	heel

C Part III:
Yellow Belt (8th kup)

Mike has a White/Yellow Belt. For the next belt he has to master a few more techniques than Kira. Besides the positions and techniques he will also learn the first exercise form as well as combinations for prearranged fighting.

First of all, he will show you a further position – the **dwit gubi**.

C

1 Position

dwit gubi (rear leg stance)

You are standing in the **moa sogi** position. Now place one foot out sideways. The other foot slides forward a little until there is a gap of one and half shoulder widths between the feet. Both knees are bent. Most (70 %) of the weight of the body is over the rear leg. There is only so much (30 %) weight of the body on the front leg, allowing you to be able to lift the leg up at anytime. The upper body and the hips are turned sideways.

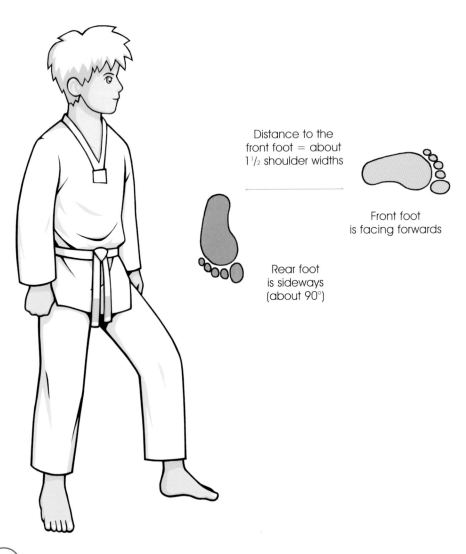

Distance to the front foot = about 1 ¹/₂ shoulder widths

Front foot is facing forwards

Rear foot is sideways (about 90°)

2   Foot Techniques

Mike learns the foot technique **dolyo chagi** (the semi-circular kick also called the 'roundhouse' kick). Just as **ap chagi** is a snapping kick, **dolyo chagi** is the same (unlike the foot kick in the **yop chagi** where the leg is not kicked out, but is pushed out to the extreme) except that it is done in a semi-circle coming in from the side.

dolyo chagi (semi-circular (roundhouse) kick)

Just like in the **ap chagi**, you bring the bent rear leg forwards, but from a position wider out until the knee is pointing at the target. The toes and instep are tensed. You now kick out with the lower leg until the leg is almost stretched out. You hit the target with the ball of the foot (**ap chuk**). After that you pull the lower leg right back and place the foot down forwards. Pay attention that while you are kicking, the foot of the standing leg twists round.

3   Defense Techniques

Just like Kira, Mike has learnt several defense techniques for the White Belt, which are carried out with a clenched fist. Now, for the Yellow Belt, he learns how to carry out these techniques with the edge of the hand.

The edge of the hand (han sonnal)

All the defense techniques with the hand, which you learnt for the White Belt, can be done with the edge of the hand. Here, you don't defend against attacks with the forearm, but deliberately with the edge of the hand. For this the hand is open, the fingers are stretched out and tensed so that the muscle on the outside edge of the hand is tensed. The thumb is held by the side of the fingers.

C

han sonnal – the edge of the hand

The swinging back movements are just like they are in other blocking actions except that the hand is open. The other hand, not involved in the defense, is kept as a clenched fist and is brought onto the hip.

The Korean names for defense with the edge of the hand are somewhat different:

hechyo arae makki changes to
sonnal hechyo arae makki

arae makki changes to
han sonnal arae makki

olgul makki changes to
han sonnal olgul makki

pakkat palmok momdang an makki changes to
han sonnal momdang an makki

pakkat palmok momdang pakkat makki changes to
han sonnal momdong pakkat makki

Besides these variations, Mike has to learn two new defense techniques. The first one is practiced first of all with a closed fist and then as the edge of the hand variation.

pakkat palmok momdong goduro pakkat makki
(reinforced forearm block)

You are standing in the **dwit gubi** position and pull both of your arms back. The back of the fist of the rear arm as well as the inside of the fist of the forward arm are facing upwards. Both arms are then brought forward at the same time. The forward arm executes a **pakkat palmok momdong pakkat makk**i. The rear arm is brought in front of the solar plexus (that is just about where the emblem is sewn onto the chest front of your **dobok**). Finally, both of the fists are turned over.

The same technique using the edge of the hand is called: **sonnal momdong pakkat makk**i.

c

an pakkat palmok momdong pakkat makki (middle zone outwards block with the inside of the forearm)

You are standing in the **dwit gubi** position. The rear arm is brought angled across in front of the upper body. The forward arm is brought forward and upwards and outwards from the middle of the body until the fist is at shoulder height. In the end position you are looking at the inside of the fist. The rear arm is brought back onto the hip.

4   Attack Techniques

palkup dolyo chiki (semi-circular elbow strike)

You are standing in the **ap gubi** position and bring the elbow of the rear arm in a semi-circle forwards up to head height. The other arm is brought back onto the hip. At the end you have to turn the hands over.

C

dung jumok olgul ape chiki (back of the fist punch at the head)

You swing back the forward arm onto the opposite shoulder from the **ap gubi** position. The side of the hand with the thumb is facing towards the shoulder. The other arm is in front of the chest. The forward arm is brought forward at head height, and turned over so that the back of the fist (**dung jumok**) is pointing forwards. You hit the target with the knuckles of the fore and middle finger. At the same time the other arm is brought back onto the hip and, as always, finally turned over.

han sonnal olgul pakkat chiki
(outward strike with the edge of the hand)

In a new attack technique is the attack is done outwards with the edge of the hand. You are standing in the **ap gubi** position. The forward arm is brought over the opposite shoulder. The open palm of the hand is pointing towards the head. The other arm is **stretched out** forwards with the back of the fist facing upwards. The edge of the hand is now swung outwards to strike the neck (mok), while at the same time the other arm is brought back onto the hip.

C

5 Exercise Form – The 4-Sided Hit (saju jirugi)

Now, there is only one exercise form required for Mike to be able to take part in the 8th **kup** grading test. A particular form or poomsae as it is known is a laid down sequence of movements for defense and attack that takes place without a partner. One has to imagine an opponent.

The exercise form for the Yellow Belt test is called the 4-Sided Hit **(saju jirugi)**. It is not yet a proper **taeguk** form, but a preparatory exercise for it.

The **saju jirugi** is, unlike the later **taeguk** forms, laid out as a crossover form. For this you practice combining two techniques – the block to the lower zone **(arae makki)** and the punch **(jumok jirugi)** as well as placing the feet down and making a 90° turn. The combination of the techniques is completed in each of four directions – hence we call it the 4-Sided Hit!

In the diagram (on the next page) you will see the individual directions as well as your start position (the figure in the middle) that should also be your end position when the exercise is correctly carried out. To make things clear, 'left' we have marked with the color red and 'right' blue. The diagram will help you in the descriptions to know which direction you are standing when doing a technique or in which direction you should be turning to next. At the back of the book in the appendix you will find another copy that you can remove.

The 4-Sided Hit Diagram

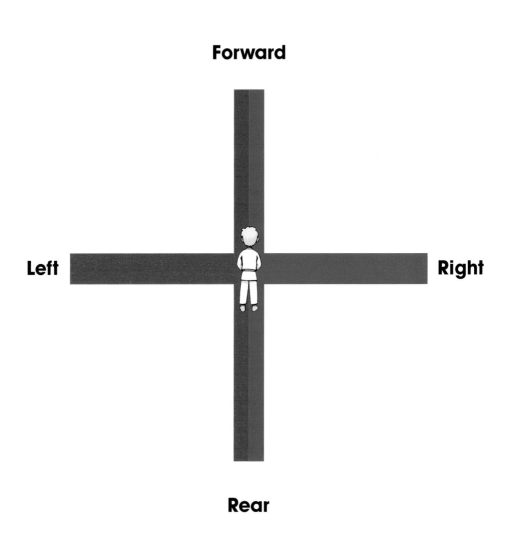

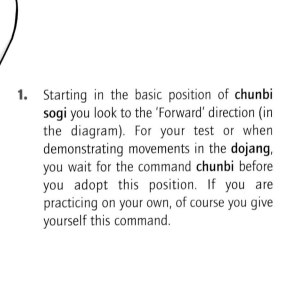

Off we go!

Mike will show you the individual steps of the 4-Sided Hit (**saju jirugi**) that he has learnt for his next test. Join in!

1. Starting in the basic position of **chunbi sogi** you look to the 'Forward' direction (in the diagram). For your test or when demonstrating movements in the **dojang**, you wait for the command **chunbi** before you adopt this position. If you are practicing on your own, of course you give yourself this command.

2. On the command **sijak** ('Begin!') you move the right leg back and place the foot down in the long step forward (**ap gubi**) position. At the same time you carry out the lower zone blocking action (**arae makki**) with the left arm as a defense technique. You are standing facing the direction of 'Forward' for this.

3. Take a step forward with the right leg and place it down in an **ap gubi** position. At the same time you carry out a punch forwards (**jumok jirugi**). You are still facing the direction of 'Forward'.

C

4. Now you turn 90° to the left. Swivel round on your left foot (the rear one) into the direction of 'Left' and place your right foot back into the **ap gubi** position. As at the beginning, you do the defensive movement of **arae makki** with the left arm (compare the sketch with Point 2 earlier).

5. Adopt the **ap gubi** position going in the direction of 'Left' again and execute a **jumok jirugi** with the right fist (see the sketch with Point 3).

6. Like in Point 4, do a 90° turn to the left so that you are now facing the direction of 'Rear'. The right leg is placed back again in the **ap gubi** position and a you execute a left **arae makki**.

7. Adopt the position of **ap gubi** in the direction of 'Rear' and execute a right-fisted punch (**jumok jirugi**).

8. Turn once again 90° to the left, this time into the direction of 'Right' as in the diagram. Place the foot into the **ap gubi** position and execute an **arae makki** with the left arm.

9. For the last movement, adopt the position of right-legged **ap gubi** and a right-handed **jumok jirugi**. As you do this last technique, you let out the **kihap** cry.

10. You now wait for the command **guman** before you adopt the final position. To do this, swivel on the left foot in the direction of 'Forward' and pull the right foot up and place it in the **pyonhi sogi chunbi** position. The movement for **guman** is slower than for **chunbi**, but you concentrate on it just as much. The final position you adopt is the same as for the **chunbi**.

You have now completed a full **saju jirugi**. If everything didn't work out straightaway – doesn't matter. Until you can do the 4-Sided Hit perfectly, you will have to practice a lot. After all everyone has to go through a learning phase.

C

Exercise

Practice the 4-Sided Hit until you can do it perfectly and smoothly. Once you have mastered it, try to do it once or twice in the opposite direction. You will note that at the beginning this is quite difficult. As you do it, instead of moving back with the right leg, use the left leg and do a right **arae makki**. You then move forward with the left foot and do a left-fisted **jumok jirugi**. Then you swivel this time 90° on the right foot instead of left (i.e., in the direction of 'Right'). Repeat the steps and techniques (right **arae makki**, left **jumok jirugi**) and move each time round to the right until you are in the **chunbi sogi** position facing 'Forward', having gone through the **guman** step (i.e., you pull the left foot up).

Of course, you don't have to do the 4-Sided Hit in the opposite direction for your test. However, by doing it this way you practice your coordination and it is a good way to prepare for the **taeguk** forms later on, where left and right turns are done.

6 Prearranged Fighting

In 'prearranged' fighting, the manner in which the attack and defense are done is laid down beforehand. You have the one-step **(hanbon gyorugi)**, two-step **(dubon gyorugi)** and the three-step **(sebon gyorugi)** fighting actions. In this book, we only describe the one-step action, because, in defense, the others are the same. Naturally, there are innumerous attack and defense variations. The variations described here are however not mandatory. It is possible that in your club or school, other variations are done. Nevertheless, it is always firmly laid down who does the attacking and who does the defending.

The attacker (here Farid: 7th **kup**) is standing opposite and an arms length away from the defender – Mike. After the greeting, Farid adopts a **chunbi sogi** with a cry (**kihap**). This way, Farid indicates his readiness to attack. The defender – Mike – also moves into a chunbi sogi with a **kihap**, and this signals to Farid that he can carry out his attack. The attacker now moves forward one step into an **ap gubi** position and attacks the middle of the defender's body with the right fist (**jumok jirugi**).

In some schools or clubs, the attacker goes back with the right first of all into the long step forward **ap gubi** position and then executes a lower zone block **(arae makki)** before he starts the attack.

1. Mike goes back with his right leg into an **ap gubi** position and defends with a left **pakkat palmok momdong pakkat makki**. With the other arm, he then executes a counterattack at Farid's head using a **jumok olgul jirugi**.

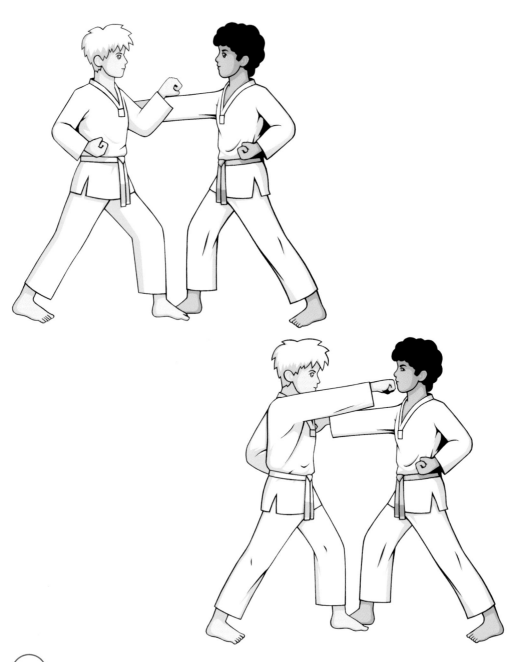

2. Mike goes back with his left leg into a **kima sogi** position and executes a right **pakkat palmok momdong an makki**. The left hand grabs hold of the attacker's right wrist. As Mike pulls the arm back towards him, he delivers a **han sonnal pakkat mok chiki** strike with the right hand at the right hand side of the attacker's neck.

C

3. Farid attacks with a **jumok olgul jirugi**. Mike goes back with his right leg into an **ap gubi** position and defends with a left **olgul makki**, attacking Farid with a right **jumok momdong jirugi**.

4. Mike goes back with his right leg into an **ap gubi** position and defends with a left **pakkat palmok momdong an makki**. He glides his left foot forward and delivers a right-arm **palkup momdong dolyo chiki** (semi-circular elbow strike) at the lower ribs.

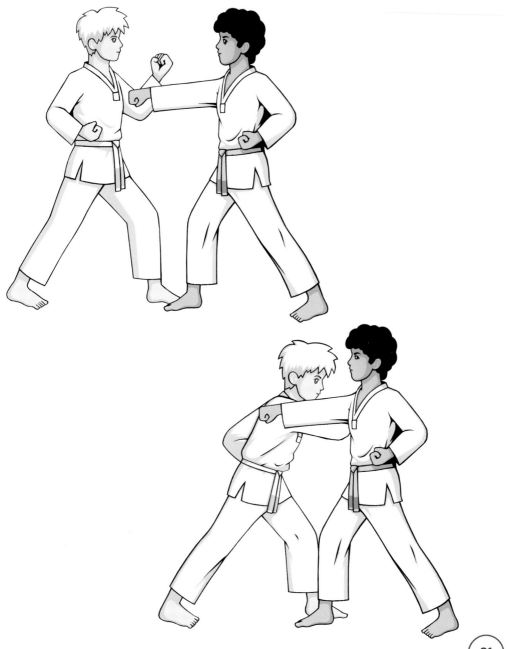

C

7 Korean Terminology III

dwit gubi	rear leg stance
dolyo chagi	semi-circular (roundhouse) kick
sonnal hechyo arae makki	double-handed wedge block with the edge of the hand in the lower zone
han sonnal	edge of the hand
han sonnal arae makki	block with the edge of the hand in the lower zone
han sonnal olgul makki	block with the edge of the hand in the upper zone
han sonnal momdong pakkat makki	outwards block with the edge of the hand
han sonnal momdong an makki	inwards block with edge of the hand
pakkat palmok momdong goduro pakkat makki	reinforced forearm block
sonnal momdong pakkat makki	double-handed defense with edge of the hand
an pakkat palmok momdong pakkat makki	middle zone outwards block with the inside of the forearm
palkup dolyo chiki	semi-circular elbow strike
dung jumok	back of the fist
dung jumok olgul ape chiki	back of the fist punch at the head
han sonnal olgul pakkat chiki	outward strike with the edge of the hand
mok	neck
hanbon gyorugi	one-step fighting action
dubon gyorugi	two-step fighting action
sebon gyorugi	three-step fighting action
saju jirugi	the 4-Sided Hit

D Part IV:
Yellow/Green Belt (7ᵗʰ kup)

1 Foot Techniques

momdolyo yop chagi (rotating sideways foot kick)

In the **dwit gubi** position, you turn the forward foot inwards and pull the rear leg up. At the same time you turn your upper body together with the lifted leg round to the rear until the area you are aiming your foot at is the same as where you were originally looking. You then kick out with the leg like in a **yop chagi**. At the end you pull it back again and place the foot down forward so that you are in the **dwit gubi** position again.

The prefix **momdolyo** means that the movement is done from a rotating turn. Later, you will meet other rotating techniques that you will recognize from the word **momdolyo**.

In preparation for free fighting (**gyorugi**), Joanne trains a lot with the punch glove. For this, the positioning of the feet is altered for two-footed techniques so that the partner is not injured and so that you can achieve a longer range. Regarding free fighting, you will learn more about this at a later date (see Taekwondo Kids Volume 2).

Punch Glove

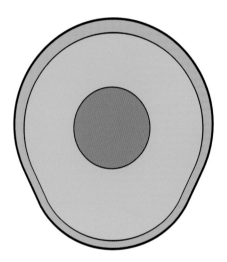

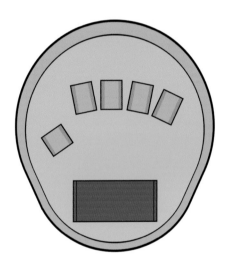

Front – Target area   Rear side – Grip

paltung chagi (semi-circular instep kick)

The **paltung chagi** is executed the same way as the **dolyo chagi** except now the instep and the toes are not tensed up but stretched out. The strike is done with the instep **(paltung)**.

naeryo chagi (kick upwards) with the sole of the foot

Just like a 'normal' **naeryo chagi**, first of all the outstretched leg is swung up straight. As it comes up, the foot is pulled outwards a little. The instep is also stretched out as in the **paltung chagi**. The strike is done with the sole of the foot **(balbadak)**.

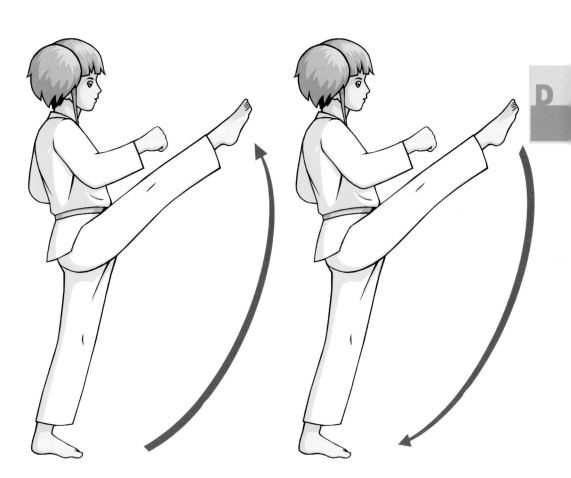

D

The first of 8 forms (**poomsae**) that you learn on the way to your first Master Grade (**poom** or **dan**) is the **taeguk il jang**. It is associated, as are the other student forms **(taeguk)**, with a **I Ging symbol** (see above), which has a meaning of the heavens. The heavens are associated in Asiatic mythology with the Beginning, Creation and Growth. With the Yellow Belt or Yellow/Green Belt you have left the level of the novice. You are standing at the beginning of serious learning and your ability and you yourself will begin to grow further. The symbol is there to remind you of this.

90

In Asia, the I Ging is known as an ancient oracle or book of wisdom. It is also called the book of change and it provides explanations for several things in the world.

In connection with the exercise forms, **tae** means 'size' and **guk** means 'eternity'. Put together, these two terms express the never-ending eternity that has no form and that is without a beginning or an end and is responsible for the origin of all beings. **Jang** is translated as 'period' or 'task'.

Just like with the 4-Sided Hit, the colored diagram (see next page: **taeguk** Diagram) should also help you with the exercises. Differently to the 4-Sided Hit diagram, this one is not in the form of a cross, it is laid out on three levels. Perhaps you have already noticed that the three levels of the **taeguk** are the same three levels as depicted in the I Ging symbol. This is also the case in all further student levels.

So that you don't have to keep leafing through the book to find the diagram, once again in the Appendix there is a pull out copy. Just cut the page out with scissors and then you have the diagram to hand whenever you need it.

Poomsae-Diagram

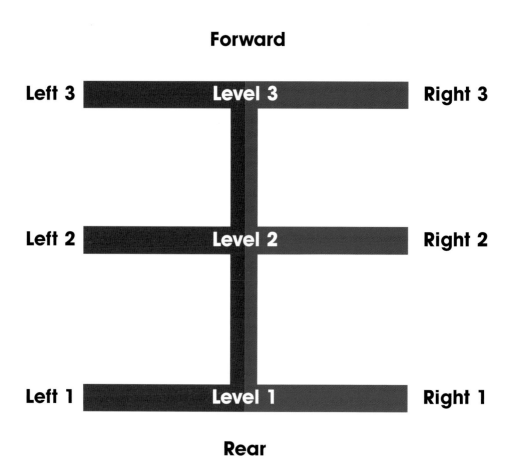

Forward

Left 3	Level 3	Right 3
Left 2	Level 2	Right 2
Left 1	Level 1	Right 1

Rear

In the **taeguk il jang**, you practice the coordination of the lower zone block **(arae makki)** and the punch **(jumok jirugi)** already used as techniques in the 4-Sided Hit actions. Some new techniques are now added – the upper zone block **(olgul makki)**, the inwards block using the outer side of the forearm **(pakkat palmok an makki)** and the forward kick **(ap chagi)**. These techniques are practiced in the short step forward position **(ap sogi)** and the long step forward position **(ap gubi)**.

On the next few pages, Joanne will show you the individual techniques for the **taeguk il jang** that you need for your 7th **kup** (Yellow/Green) grading test.

So that you have a better overview, the individual exercise sequences are broken down into sections. These refer to each Level (1,2 and 3) in the diagram pattern you are moving in. A new section begins each time that you move onto another level. Your starting position is on Level 1 looking in the direction of 'Forward'.

D

Section 1: Level 1

1. The command **chunbi** has been given so you are standing in the **chunbi sogi** position.

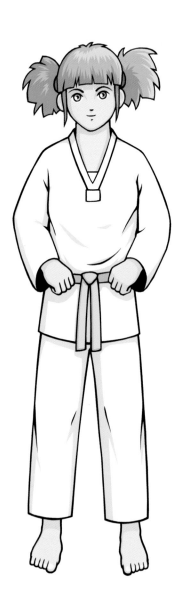

2. On the command **sijak** you swivel round on your right foot to the left in the direction of 'Left 1' in the diagram. To do this, first of all you turn your head to the left and then turn the right foot in to the left, placing the left foot into the short step forward position (**ap sogi**). At the same time you execute the lower zone block (**arae makki**) as a defensive technique.

3. Move forward one step with the right foot into the **ap sogi** position. At the same time you execute a forward punch **(jumok jirugi)** at the middle of the body **(momdong)**. You are still facing the direction of 'Left 1' (see the diagram).

4. Now turn round 180° to face the direction of 'Right 1'. Remember, the turn always starts by moving the head and is then followed by the body. Swivel on the left foot and place the right one in front of the left foot in the direction of 'Right 1' in an **ap sogi** position. As you place the foot down you execute an **arae makki** with the right arm.

D

11. Place your right foot forward in the direction of 'Left 2' in an **ap sogi** position. You again execute a **jumok momdong jirugi** with the left arm.

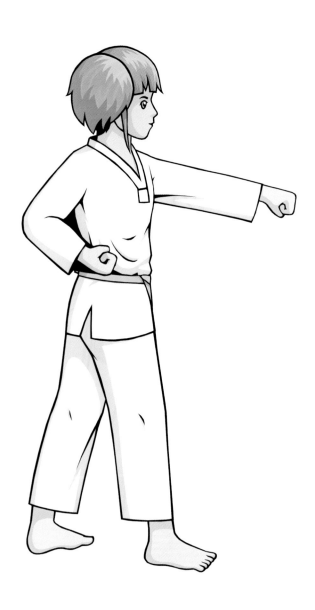

12. Now swivel round on the left foot to the right in the direction of 'Forward'. Place your right foot in front of the left one in an **ap gubi** position and execute an **arae makki** block with the arm on the side of the right foot.

D

13. Stay standing in the **ap gubi** position and immediately after doing the **arae makki** execute a left-fisted **jumok momdong jirugi**. As you do it let out a loud **kihap** cry.

As before, your forward foot is now already, to all purposes, in the next level. As soon as you pull your rear foot up to the forward one with the next step, you are now completely inside Level 3.

Section 3: Level 3

14. Swivel round on the right foot to the left in the direction of 'Left 3' and place your foot down forward in the **ap sogi** position. As you do this execute a block to the upper zone **(olgul makki)** with the left arm.

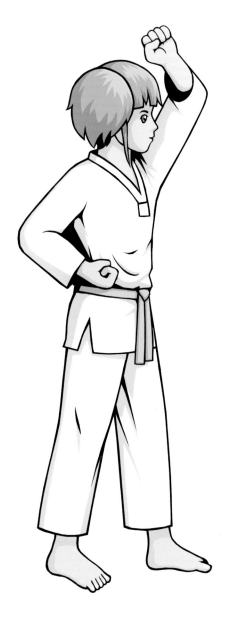

15. From this position you now execute a forward kick **(ap chagi)** still moving in the direction of 'Left 3'.

16. After the kick, place the foot down in the short step forward position **(ap sogi)** and execute a right-fisted **jumok momdong jirugi**.

D

17. Swivel round on the left foot to the right in the direction of 'Right 3' and place the right foot down in front of the left foot in an **ap sogi** position. Execute an **olgul makki** with the right arm.

18. Now follows an **ap chagi** again, this time with the left leg in the direction of 'Right 3'.

D

19. After the kick, place the left leg in front of the right leg in an **ap sogi** position and carry out a **jumok momdong jirugi** with the left fist.

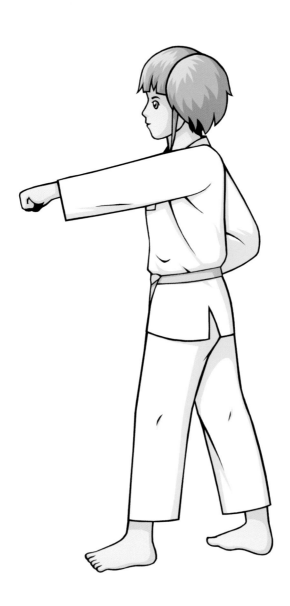

Section 4: The "Way back"

20. You now begin the "way back" that will lead you into a final position at the end in 'Level 1'. Swivel on the right foot 90° to the right in the direction of 'Rear' in the diagram. Place your left foot in front of the right foot in an **ap gubi** position (long step forward). Carry out the technique of **arae makki** with the left.

21. Take another step forward with the right leg in the direction of 'Rear' into an **ap gubi** position. As you do this you carry out a right-fisted **jumok jirugi** to the middle zone **(momdong)**. As you do the fist stroke you let out a kihap cry. The "way back" is now completed. Wait in this position for the command of **guman** (finish, end of exercise) before you finish off doing the **taeguk il jang**.

22. On the command **guman** swivel round to the left on the right foot in the direction of 'Forward'. Place the left foot a shoulder width away alongside the right foot in a **chunbi sogi** position and adopt the **guman** stance in Level 1.

D

1. Farid attacks with a right-fisted **jumok momdong jirugi**. Joanne retreats into an **ap gubi** position and delivers a left **pakkat palmok momdong an makki** (block in the middle zone using the outer side of the forearm inwards). Joanne grasps Farid's right wrist with her left hand and then pulls her left foot back into an **ap sogi** position and executes a **naeryo chagi** with the right leg across Farid's arm that she is holding.

2. Joanne puts her right leg back into a **dwit gubi** position and defends using a **sonnal momdong makki**. The left hand grasps hold of Farid's right wrist followed by an **ap chagi** at Farid's right armpit. Joanne pulls him towards her as she does this.

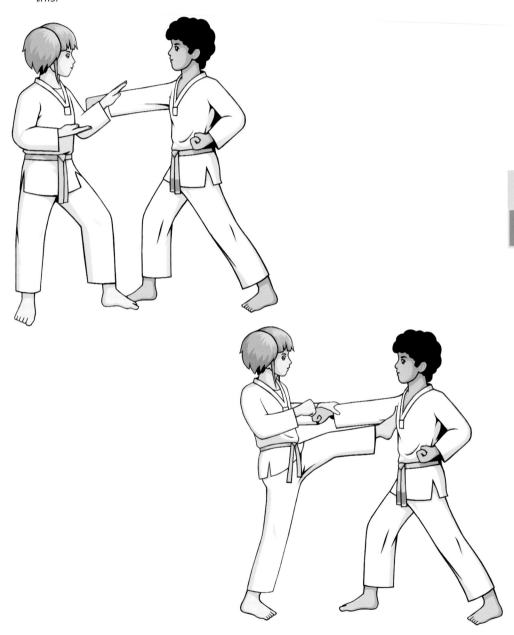

3. Joanne defends herself by placing her right leg back in a **dwit gubi** position and at the same time blocking the attack with a **palmok momdong pakkat makki**. Finally, Joanne slides back a little and delivers a **dolyo chagi** outside kick with the right leg at Farid's head.

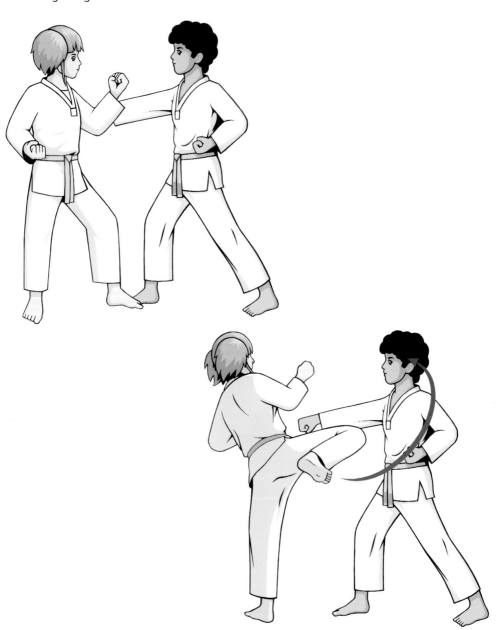

4. While Farid is attacking, Joanne slides back into a **dwit gubi** position to establish a gap between them. To cover her body she brings her fists up into a **goduro makki** stance. Finally she executes a **yop chagi** kick with the right leg at the opponent's solar plexus or head.

D

These exercises complete the program for Joanne's belt grading test. Of course, besides the new techniques she has just learnt, she continues to practice the blocks, strikes, kicks and combinations that she learnt for the White and the White/Yellow belts. This is because progress in Taekwondo doesn't only mean always learning new techniques, it also means perfecting everything that has been gone through in lessons already. A simple technique that is executed correctly has more effect than a complicated one that is incorrectly executed.

With this in mind, continue practicing your techniques – whether new or old, so that they get better and better and permit you to achieve the best possible effect with them.

4 Korean Terminology IV

momdolyo yop chagi	rotating sideways foot kick
paltung	instep of the foot
paltung chagi	semi-circular (crescent) kick with the instep
gyorugi	free fighting
balbadak	sole of the foot
poomsae	movement form or exercise form
taeguk	'size' and 'eternity'
taeguk il jang	the first form symbol – the heavens and light

D

Summary

For the time being Suko and his pals say cheerio. They have shown you all that you have to know and be able to do for your 7ᵗʰ **kup** test. By now you will know whether Taekwondo is the sport for you and whether you want to go on. Who knows? Maybe one day you will also have the Master grade belt like Suko. But keep in mind, even for a Master grade, having a practical handbook is always useful so that you are able to refer to it.

Before you close this book, have a look at the few pages in the Appendix. Here you will find all the Korean terminology in alphabetical order as well as a couple of addresses and the diagrams for the 4-Sided Hit and the first exercise form.

Have lots of fun and success in your training!

D

APPENDIX

Vocabulary

In this vocabulary are all the Korean terms that appear in this book.

Pronunciation: It is difficult to transliterate the Korean language into the Roman alphabet. Korean does not use characters – instead they use symbols. Words must therefore be pronounced phonetically. You will find various spellings for the words all over the world, but the important thing is to try to match the different sounds you hear elsewhere in other **dojangs** with the words in this list.

an pakkat palmok momdong pakkat makki	middle zone outwards block with the inside of the lower arm
ap chagi	forward kick
ap chuk	ball of the foot
ap gubi	long step forward
ap sogi	short step forward
arae	lower zone
arae makki	block in the lower zone
balbadak	sole of the foot
balnal	outside edge of the foot
bandae jirugi	punching action on the forward leg side
baro jirugi	punching action on the rear leg side
charyot kyongne	Pay attention, Greetings!
chuchum sogi	riding position, feet splayed out
chunbi	Get ready! Adopt a starting position.
dan	Master grade for grown-ups
dobok	training uniform
dojang	training hall
dolyo chagi	semi-circular kick
dubon gyorugi	two-step fighting action

dubon jirugi	double punching action
dung jumok olgul ape chiki	back of the fist punch at the head
dung jumok	back of the fist
dwit gubi	rear leg stance
dwit kumchi	heel
guman	end of the exercise, or end of being ready
gyorugi	free fighting
han sonnal	edge of the hand
han sonnal arae makki	block with the edge of the hand in the lower zone
han sonnal momdong an makki	inwards block with edge of the hand
han sonnal momdong pakkat makki	outwards block with the edge of the hand
han sonnal olgul makki	block with the edge of the hand in the upper zone
han sonnal olgul pakkat chiki	outward strike with the edge of the hand
hanbon gyorugi	one-step fighting action
hechyo arae makki	double wedge block in the lower zone
jumok jirugi	punching
kihap	attack cry
kima sogi	saddle position
kup	belt grade
makki	blocking
moa sogi	closed position
mok	neck
momdolyo yop chagi	rotating sideways foot kick
momdong	middle zone
naeryo chagi	kick upwards

olgul	upper zone
olgul makki	block in the upper zone
pakkat palmok momdong an makki	block in the middle zone using the outer side of the lower arm inwards
pakkat palmok momdong goduro pakkat makki	reinforced lower arm block
pakkat palmok momdong pakkat makki	block in the middle zone using the outer side of the lower arm outwards
palkup dolyo chiki	semi-circular elbow strike
paltung chagi	semi-circular (crescent) kick with the instep of the foot
poom	Master grade for children and youths
poomsae	movement form or exercise form
pyonhi sogi	parallel position
sabum	trainer, instructor
saju jirugi	the 4-Sided Hit
sebon gyorugi	three-step fighting action
sijak	Begin!
sonnal hechyo arae makki	double handed wedge block with the edge of the hand in the lower zone
sonnal momdong pakkat makki	double-handed defense with edge of the hand
taeguk il jang	the first form symbol – the heavens and light
taeguk	'size' and 'eternity'
ty	belt
yop chagi	sideways kick with the foot

Korean Numbers

hana	one
dul	two
set	three
net	four
dasot	five
yosot	six
ilgup	seven
yodol	eight
ahop	nine
yol	ten
sumul	twenty
sonum	thirty
mahun	forty
suin	fifty
vesun	sixty
irhun	seventy
yodun	eighty
ahun	ninety
paek	hundred
chon	thousand

Unions and Addresses

World Taekwondo Federation
F Joyang Building 113
Samseong-Dong
Gangnam-Gu
Seoul
Korea 135-090
Internet: http//www.wtf.org

Kukkiwon
635 Yuksam-Dong
Gangnam-Gu
Seoul
Korea 135-908
Internet: http//www.Kukkiwon.or.kr

We wish you lots of fun in your training!

Joanne, Farid, Suko, Kira, Mike

The 4-Sided Hit Diagram

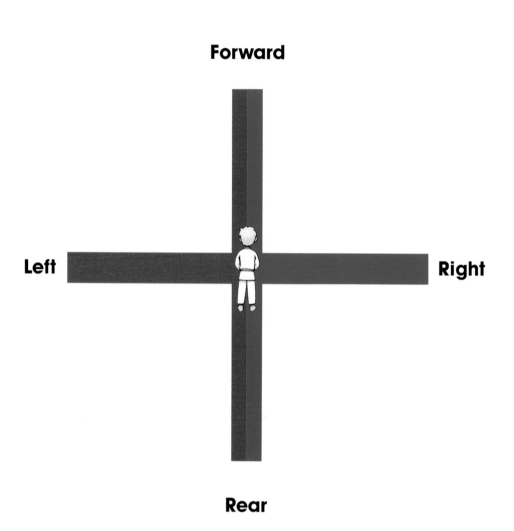

Forward

Left

Right

Rear

Poomsae-Diagram

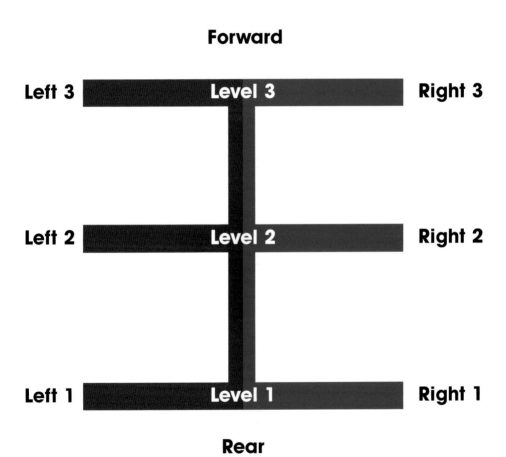

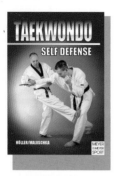

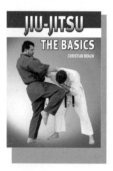
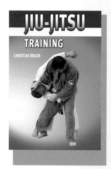
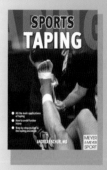

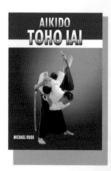